GOD, HIS PEOPLE, AND NETWORK MARKETING

BY

EDDIE TRAYLOR

LIFE TO LEGACY

Cover design by: Tasha Sykes
Legacy Designs, Inc.
Legacydesigninc@gmail.com

Published by:
Life To Legacy, LLC
(877) 267-7477
www.Life2Legacy.com

TABLE OF CONTENTS

PRESENTED TO:

Contact the author at:
Eddiet706@gmail.com

Dedication

This book is dedicated to my two sons, Louis and Eddie, and my daughter Ashanti. Also to the memory of my daddy in the Gospel who mentored me in my new walk with Christ, Apostle C.L. Jackson

INTRODUCTION

One of the hottest topics discussed among the Christian community today, is concerning money and finances. Whether it is a turnoff to some, or an attention getter to others, the subject invariably solicits a wide range of attitudes and opinions.   When it comes to the Scriptures, some treat the subject of finances as being worldly and taboo. On the other hand, some measure their level of spirituality according to the balance in their bank account. However, it should come as no surprise that the Bible has quite a bit to say about money and the Christian's relationship to it. Contrary to what some believe, God does not have an issue with people having money. However, what God does have a problem with is when money has people and not the other way around. In Matthew 6:33, here is what Jesus declared, "But seek first his kingdom and his righteousness, and all these things will be given to you as well" (NIV).

Over the years, I have observed, that many of us born-again believers are struggling financially. I'm talking about Bible-believing, Holy Spirit-filled, sincere believers. The question is, is there a disconnect between, what the Bible declares, and what is actually manifesting in people's lives? I believe that there is and are three reasons we as believers are missing the manifestation of Matthew 6:33 in our lives. The first is that this scripture is connected to other pertinent principles found through the Bible. I'll discuss that in greater detail in chapters 1, 4, and 5—scriptures that are keys to a better understanding of Matthew 6:33.

The second reason is that we don't ask God for wisdom to understand this scripture. Instead, we take it for granted that since it is a simple statement, we don't need God's direction and wisdom to interpret the meaning correctly. Clearly, there is a lack of understanding because millions of believers in the United States and all over the world suffer at the hands of poverty. Third, and finally, is that we feel that the promise of Matthew 6:33 is automatic, and all we have to do is wait and do nothing. However, there are two operative words in that passage, "seek" and "added." You can sit around waiting. You should be seeking. Without *seeking*, God will be doing no *adding*.

In the sixth chapter of Matthew, Jesus spoke much against the impact materialism can have on one's life, and ultimately the relationship one has with the Lord. He told the disciples, do not worry about what you will eat or what clothes you will wear. These things merely gratify the body but have no spiritual significance. Jesus knew that it is easier for a person to trust in the things their five senses can perceive. But just as He did with His disciples, He challenges us to seek the greater more important principles on how the Kingdom of God operates. Therefore He put the priority on seeking first the Kingdom of God and its righteousness, which put a person in a much better position to have God add the material things that our hearts also desire.

CHAPTER 1

SOLOMON, WISDOM, AND WEALTH

Examples are important. When it comes to obtaining and managing riches and wealth, it is imperative to examine how those who achieved success did it. So often we want to reinvent the wheel. However, we must ask ourselves, "What is the thought process that got them where they are?" Once we learn what methods and strategies were used and the thought process behind it was, then we will discover it's not magic, or mere good luck, but in many cases, it is an observable repeatable process that can be followed by others. There is only one way to make a jet that will fly. There are certain aerodynamic principles that must be followed, or your jet will never leave the ground. Similarly, so it is with finances when it comes to the accumulation and maintenance of wealth.

In 1 Kings 3:5-15, NIV, is the account of God appearing to Solomon in a dream, and said, "ask for whatever you want me to give you." Wow, think of that. God show up in your bedroom and inviting you to ask Him for anything you wanted. There is a whole list of things the average person would have asked for such as health, wealth, and the riddance of opposition. But Solomon didn't ask for any of these things. Solomon asked for wisdom in order that he might judge righteously over God's people.

Solomon's request pleased God and it was granted. God gave him unparalleled wisdom, but God also blessed him with the things he didn't ask for—riches. Therefore, not only was Solomon the wisest man in the world, but God made him the richest in the world as well. It is clear; asking for wisdom was the determining factor in the level of blessing bestowed upon Solomon. For this reason, I believe that wisdom is the missing ingredient in the recipe for the success that many are trying to achieve. This is why seeking first the Kingdom of God and its righteousness, opens the door for God to do the adding. Trust me, God adds better than you or me.

Wisdom tells believers everywhere, if we listen, that we are not supposed to sit up, fold our hands, and simply wait for food, something to drink, and clothes to come to us. God wants us to know that He has His part (the keeping of His promise). And, we have our part (the seeking and implementation of wisdom). Whether it's government assistance, a job, or acquiring a business, an effective plan and strategy has to be developed by a knowledgeable person in order to acquire necessities and accumulate wealth.

Now, then, let's get back to the food, clothes, and drink question. Yes, Matthew 6:33 talks only about the necessities of life; food, clothes, and something to drink. I can't imagine what life would be without a cup of coffee in the morning or a glass of pineapple juice with my pancakes and eggs when I visit the restaurant. Today, our list of necessities is longer than it was two thousand years ago. Let's take a look at an average 21^{s}t century family's list: food, clothes, drink (water, juice, coffee, tea, etc.), mortgage or rent, electricity, gas (heating), television service, cell phones, refrigerator, stove, church donations, taxes, life insurance, health insurance, transportation (automobile or public), credit cards, and internet service. Whew!

We didn't mention savings accounts, which would supply money for emergencies that pop up, such as refrigerator or car breakdowns. Having cash on hand for unexpected events like this helps us to avoid credit-card or personal-loan debt. If you or I struggle to pay our normal expenses, and there is nothing left to contribute to our own personal emergency savings fund, that is not good. Suppose we lose our job or our business income declines? Wouldn't it be wonderful to have three to six month's savings in the bank to pay our expenses until the financial challenge we are experiencing is over?

If as a member of the kingdom of God, you don't mind struggling and living from paycheck to paycheck—well that's on you. When you depart from this life here on Earth, you will get to heaven because Jesus promised us, as members, eternal life. However, if you know you seek the kingdom of God and his righteousness daily, but you feel that Matthew 6:33 is not being manifested in your life as it should be, then the message in the following chapters of this book is for you. James 1:5 says, "If any of you lacks wisdom, he should ask

God, who gives generously to all without finding fault, and it will be given to him" (NIV).

My prayer is that in the coming chapters of this book, God will give you a discerning and understanding heart concerning His wisdom and the coming wave of wealth that I believe is about to sweep across the Body of Christ both as individuals and as the church.

CHAPTER 2

FINANCE AND BUSINESS IN THE CHURCH

In the Book of Acts, two very important incidents occurred at the church of Jerusalem. The first one is described in the passage below.

> And all that believed were together, and had all things common; and sold their possessions and goods, and parted them [gave the proceeds in money] to all men [everyone], as every man [they all] had need. And they continuing daily with one accord in the temple, and breaking bread from house to house, did eat their meat with gladness and singleness of heart, praising God, and having favor with all people. And the Lord added to the church daily such as should be saved.
>
> Acts 2:44-47, KJV (emphasis mine)

The second incident is from the fourth chapter of Acts, it reads,

> And the multitude of them that believed were of one heart, and of one soul; neither said [nor claimed] of any

of them that aught of the things that he possessed was
his own; but they had all things common. And with
great power gave the apostles witness of the resurrec-
tion of the Lord Jesus: and great grace was upon them
all. Neither was there any among them that lacked:
for as many as were possessors of lands or houses sold
them, and brought the prices [money from the sales]
of the things that were sold, and laid them down at the
apostles' feet; and distribution was made unto every
man according as he had need.

Acts 4:32-35, KJV (emphasis mine)

Three words stand out in this passage, *lands, houses* and *possessors*, all of which are mentioned in the plural. However,
the word possessors is interesting, because this indicates
someone who owned multiple properties. This is comparable to business people today who own more than one property. I don't believe that people sold their only home in order to give to the poor. But by being multi-property owners
they were able to sale excess property because they were in
the position to do so. If you desire to give in this type of capacity, first you should give yourself time to acquire enough
properties so that you can afford to give one away without it
hurting you or your family.

As you can see, the first church was interested in meeting the needs of its members. How did they do it? They
brought all their resources together for the common good of
everyone. This is how they took care of the poor members
who needed help. There was no public aid, Social Secu-
rity, or food-stamp assistance programs. There was only the

church and its members taking care of their own financial needs. In the Acts 2:44 text, it was "all that believed." In the second instance, it was "as many as were possessors of lands or houses" (Acts 4:34). In the first case, they were average income earners. In the second case, they were landlords and business owners. My point is that selling, exchanging goods for money was a part of the early church's beginning. Using money from the sale of goods and property to create resources for the less fortunate was a foundational aspect of the early church.

At this point, one may suppose there is a conflict between such financial transactions and spiritual reverential aspects of church. One could make the claim against pursuing financial gain by pointing out that Jesus turned over the vendors' money change tables and chased them out of the temple with a whip. Let's examine the scripture and see what we find concerning the reason. Here are the three accounts: Matthew 21:12-13, Mark 11:15-17, and John 2:13-16.

> "And Jesus went into the temple of God, and cast out all them that sold and bought in the temple, and overthrew the tables of the moneychangers, and the seats of them that sold doves, and said to them, 'It is written, my house shall be called the house of prayer; but ye have made it a den of thieves'"   Matthew 21:12-13

In Mark, Jesus went into the temple and began to cast out them that sold and bought in the temple, and overthrew the tables of the moneychangers, and the seats of those that sold doves; and would not suffer (allow) that any man (anyone) carry any vessel (merchandise) through the temple saying, Is it not written, my house shall be called of all nations the house of prayer? But you have made it a den of thieves (Mark 11:15-17).

Finally, in John, Jesus went up to Jerusalem and found in the temple those that sold oxen and sheep and doves, and the changers of money sitting: and when he had made a scourge of small cords (whip), he drove them all out of the temple, and the sheep, and the oxen; and poured out the changers' money, and overthrew the tables; and said unto them that sold doves, take these things hence (away); make not my Father's house an house of merchandise (a place of business) (John 2:13-16).

We know that Jesus felt it was wrong to turn a place of worship into a pop up store, distracting people from focusing on worship. But what did he mean in Matt. 21:13 and Mark 16:17 when he referred, to the vendors (sellers) and customers as thieves.

Why would Jesus chase the buyers and sellers out of the temple? To begin our search for answers, let's take note of the fact that he called them "thieves." He made this accusation once in Matthew 21:13 and again in Mark 11:17. In Leviticus 22:17-33, there is a list of rules and regulations concerning the proper guidelines for the sale of sacrificial animals. They were used in family devotions and temple religious ceremonies. These animals couldn't be sick, deformed, or injured. I believe the vendors doing the selling were guilty of cheating people by selling animals that were not in good condition. Perhaps, the buyers knew that they themselves were purchasing defective sacrificial animals. In Mark 11:16, Jesus stopped some people from carrying merchandise through the temple. This was a form of distraction from worship. This angered Jesus because he wants us focused on God the Father during times of worship. In John 2:16, Jesus accused the vendors of converting the temple into a "house of merchandise [business]." There is indeed a business dimension to and of the church because every local church has expenses to be paid. However, the main two objectives of the church are the provision of a place to worship and the promotion of discipleship to the people for Jesus Christ.

I am not saying that we should convert our churches into versions of boutique shops, mini marts, or shopping malls. Nor am I advocating that businesses set up shop in the church after Sunday worship services. What I am saying is that congregations should be encouraged to support church members who are business owners and service providers. This type of support helps these businesses grow. The benefit to the church comes in the form of tithes and offerings these same business owners give back to the church. This should always be a driving principle. How is what we are doing benefiting the Kingdom of God and the church? In doing so we are fulfilling an aspect of seeking the Kingdom of God. Christians in the first century figured this out. It would behoove us today to be like minded.

As I travel throughout the city of Chicago, I've noticed more abandoned and boarded-up churches than I've ever seen before. I often wonder if it's the same in other cities and towns across America. I realize that when church members lose their job and their income, that affects their ability to give to their church offerings. But, I also see more pastors, church leaders, and lay members going into business for themselves and their family. I believe that this is the strategy of the Holy Spirit to sweep the wave of prosperity across the Body of Christ in order for the men and women of God to fulfill their vision for the Kingdom of God on Earth and a better life for more people.

CHAPTER 3

MATTHEW SUMMARIZED

Jesus' Sermon on the Mount is probably the most promi-
nent sermon found in of the Bible where many Kingdom principles are noted. One of the principles that are
key to this study is found in Matthew 6:24 (KJV), where
the Lord says, "No man can serve two masters: for either
he will hate the one, and love the other; or else he will hold
[be devote] to the one, and despise the other. Ye cannot
serve God and mammon [riches]." The NASB translates
it this way, "You cannot serve God and wealth." The reason
we shouldn't serve God and wealth at the same time is because the purpose of wealth was serve people not the other
way around. What often ends up happening, people end up
serving wealth. They wake up thinking of money.

The acquisition of money dominates their lives and is the
priority of their life. This places money in an exalted position in their hearts and that's where the problem is. Covet-
ousness is a sin and according to Colossians 3:5, covetous-
ness is idolatry. Idolatry is having another god, instead of
God. Let's not get it confused, the favor to obtain wealth
comes from God. Deuteronomy 8:18 admonishes not to
forget where your blessings come from when He says, "...

remember the Lord your God, for it is he who gives you the ability to produce wealth."

Having wealth should not automatically be seen as being antithetical to God. If talking about money was important to Jesus, it should be important to us, his followers. I believe Matthew 6:34 holds the key to why believers feel that it is not spiritual to talk about money and money-making business opportunities. Matthew 6:34 says, "Take therefore no thought for the morrow; for the morrow shall take thought for the things of itself. Sufficient unto the day is the evil thereof." Unfortunately, this is how the King James translators translated it. Their objective was to translate the original manuscripts from Greek to English. Since 1611, when their version of the Bible was completed, the English language has evolved into what we currently speak today. Some of the former English words are obsolete. Also, with the advancement of civilization in the areas of science, technology, economics, and education, many more words have been created that did not exist in that time.

Today, because of the advancement of knowledge and the evolution of the English language, scholars have been able to produce more accuracy from the original manuscripts of the Bible. For instance, the NASB says, "Do not worry about tomorrow, for tomorrow will take care of itself. Each day has enough trouble of its own." The NIV says, "Therefore do not worry about tomorrow, for tomorrow will worry about itself. Each day has enough trouble of its own."

The difference between the modern versions and the King

James is the difference in saying "Don't worry about tomorrow" as opposed to saying "Take therefore no thought about tomorrow." In other words, the King James Version is saying, "Don't think about tomorrow." The difference can seem to be deceptive but that was not King James and the translators' goal. However, they were handicapped by a limited access to Greek manuscripts from where the English versions derive. On the other hand, in modern versions, scholars had the advantage having access to better Greek manuscripts which had not been discovered in the 17th century when the King James Version was commissioned. Consequently, modern translators were able to produce a more accurate meaning for those of us that speak English, a language that did not exist in Jesus day. Therefore, we now know that Jesus was telling us not to worry to the extent that anxiety controls us. In Philippians, Paul is clear when he writes, "be anxious for nothing..."(Phil. 4:6).

From this we can understand that it is not sinful to think, plan, strategize, and pursue financial knowledge and corresponding activities for future financial gain. If we examine the sixth chapter of the Book of Matthew, we will see that Jesus started talking about material things (things that require money to obtain) in verse 19 and then temporarily ends the subject two verses later in verse 21. After talking about "light" and "darkness" in verses 22 and 23, he resumes his conversation about "money" in verse 24 and continues until the end of the chapter in verse 34 for a total of fourteen verses. Previously in his conversation, he talked about "giving" in verses 1 to 4 (four verses); "prayer" in verses 5-13 (nine verses); "forgiveness" in verses 14-15 (two verses); and, "fasting" in verses 16-18 (three verses).

I believe Jesus spoke so much about obtaining material things because He knew that in generations to come, after he finished his earthly ministry, there would be lots of confusion concerning our attitude toward money and materialism. Christ is more concerned about us seeking the kingdom of God and His righteousness, and let God do the adding. As stated in Deut. 8:18, it is God that gives us the power to obtain wealth. As long as we keep our priorities straight, we are better positioned for kingdom principles to manifest in our lives.

You are now at a point in this book where it is important for you to decide whether you should read it all the way through. If you've already decided to continue this journey of expanding your knowledge, I ask you to stay committed. I believe that because you are taking an active part in your accumulation of Godly knowledge in this book, God Himself will stir up the wisdom already inside of you and grant you even more.

In Steven Covey's book, *The 7 Habits of Highly Effective People*, he lists "proaction" (action applied to getting something done) as the first habit or step to getting something done. In order to be effective in anything, you have to take action and do something. This includes obtaining a better understanding of scripture. I commend you for obtaining this book and reading it. Because of it, you are putting yourself in position to receive of the wave of financial abundance that God has already started sweeping across and into the Body of Christ—the church.

Please allow me to reiterate something I said before in chapter 1. If you don't mind living from paycheck to paycheck, and you are a Christian, you are going to get to heaven when you depart from this life here on Earth. This will happen whether you are poor of wealthy. If you are one of the millions of believers like me who believe that the abundant life Jesus talked about in John 10:10, where He speaks of the "abundant life" can include finances, then get ready to be blessed. Therefore, if you are tired of plain, ordinary, normal, status-quo living, you need not to feel guilty about having the desire for more for yourself and your family. In the next chapter, we will look at the life of two rich men and see which one honored God in his heart.

CHAPTER 4

A BUSINESSMAN AND JESUS

I would like to mention two rich men from the Bible. The first one's name is not recorded. His story is in Luke 18:18-23. "And a certain ruler asked him, saying, Good master, what shall I do to inherit eternal life?" And, Jesus said unto him. "Why callest thou me good? None is good, save one, that is God. Thou knowest the commandments. Do not commit adultery. Do not kill, do not steal, do not bear false witness, Honor thy father and mother?" And, he said, "All these I have kept from my youth up." Now, when Jesus heard these things, he said unto him, "Yet lackest thou one thing: sell all that thou hast and distribute unto the poor, and thou shalt have treasure in heaven: and come, follow me." And, when he heard this, he was very sorrowful: for he was very rich. The second one is named Zaccheus (Luke 19:1-8).

Most people think of the first rich man with the unrecorded name when it comes to remembering rich people recorded in the Bible. He turned down an opportunity to follow Jesus because his wealth was in control of him. He refused to give up his status, possessions, and money because he valued them more than he valued fellowship and a relationship with Jesus. However, the second rich man, whose name was Zaccheus, saw things differently. Even though he was rich and had lots of goods and money, he wasn't in love with them as the first rich man was. What's interesting about this man is that he was a publican (tax collector). He was probably a type of supervisor because he was "...the chief among publicans, and he was rich." He found time between working for the Roman government and his personal activities to run a successful business.

Luke 19:1-10 says, And he sought to see Jesus who he was; and could not for the press because he was of little stature. And, he ran before, and climbed up into a sycamore tree to see him; for he was to pass that way. And when Jesus came to the place, he looked up, and saw him, and said unto him, "Zaccheus, make haste, and come down: For today, I must abide at thy house." And, he made haste, and came down, and received him joyfully. And when they saw it, they all murmured, saying that he was going to be guest with a man that is a sinner. And Zaccheus stood, and said unto the Lord; "Behold, Lord, the half of my goods I give to the poor; and if I have taken anything from any man by false accusation, I restore him four-fold." And, Jesus said unto him, "This day is salvation come to this house, for so much as he also is a son of Abraham. For the Son of man is come to seek and to save that which was lost."

Here are four principles that were evident in the life of Zaccheus:

1) When it comes to starting your day, be aggressive when it comes to having some intimate time with Jesus in prayer, meditation, and Bible study. Whether it's ten minutes or an hour, do it, and you'll be better prepared to face whatever confronts you that day. Zaccheus knew he had to see Jesus's face, and he was too short to see him in the crowd; so, because he was determined, a plan came to him right on time.

2) Have a heart and mind open and available to help someone in need. Zaccheus knew there were some poor people in town; so, while there in the presence of Jesus, he decided to give goods to sell (half of his business) so some poor people could eat. Sometimes, it's as simple as a smile, a handshake, a helping hand, or hug.

3) In your interactions with people, never be ashamed to say, "I'm sorry" when you are wrong. This is what Zaccheus was demonstrating when he restored money to the people he had fraudulently taken if from (Luke 19:8).

4) Always be grateful. Being in a continual state of gratitude promotes joy, peace, and good health in you. Zaccheus climbed down from the tree joyfully (Luke 19:6) because he was grateful that Jesus had singled him out in the midst of the crowd—up in a tree.

Jesus knew that the critics hated Zaccheus because he was a so-called flunky working for the Roman government. He was also despised because he was rich. I believe Jesus admired Zaccheus because rich or poor, black or white, young or old, with God it's the condition of the heart that matters. So, if people are down on you and critical of you and you know you're doing everything you can to please the Lord, remember and meditate on this verse, "And let us not get weary in well-doing: for in due season we shall reap if we faint not" (Galatians 6:9).

CHAPTER 5

PAUL, THE MINISTER AND ENTREPRENEUR

Most people, when they think of Paul, think of him as a missionary, an apostle, a preacher, an author, a teacher, a leader, a scholar, or a disciple. Indeed, he was all those things. However, very few if any think of Paul as an entrepreneur. Webster's Compact Dictionary says an entrepreneur is "one who organizes a business undertaking, assuming the risk for the sake of the profit." Acts 18:1-3 states,

> After these things, he [Paul] left Athens and went to Corinth. And, they found a Jew named Aquila, a native of Pontus, having recently come from Italy with his wife, Priscilla...and because he was of the same trade, he stayed with them and they were working, for by trade they were tentmakers. (NASB)

It is of equal value to realize that he had a business dimension added by God to his life-style. Concerning Paul's character, purpose, and destiny, his business ability helped him to achieve the success of his ministry of advancing the kingdom of God and helping its people to gain knowledge of Christ.

Let's take a look at his own words concerning this matter in scripture.

For you yourselves know how you ought to follow our example, because we did not act in an undisciplined manner among you nor did we eat anyone's bread [food] without paying for it, but with labor and hardship we kept working night and day so that we would not be a burden [financially] to any of you; not because we do not have the right to this, but in order to offer ourselves as a model to you, so that you would follow our example. 2 Thessalonians 3:7-9 (Emphasis mine)

Paul is not saying that pastors and evangelists should not receive salary or donations from congregations. He is simply saying that in this instance, he chose, as a businessman, to pay for his own expenses. This is an option that a business owner with incoming business revenue who pastors or evangelizes has.

The validity of my reasoning that Paul was an entrepreneur lies in the fact that the money he earned in this instance came from the profits he made selling the tents that he produced. Am I saying that every apostle, pastor, or evangelist should be a business owner? Of course, not. However, I am saying that successful entrepreneurship as a dimension of any pastor's or evangelist's life would be an asset to their family, to the congregation they serve, to themselves, and to the body of Christ in general.

As we covered in Chapter 3, your expenses would be paid if you decide to retire from the ministry. If you have properly invested some of your business income, you can then live comfortably as opposed to living in poverty after retiring.

Think of all the retirees that you see today who are forced to work a part-time job just to make ends meet.

When God chooses a person for a certain position, He uses the qualities, talents, gifts, and skills that that person already has and refines them for use in the kingdom of God. It's no accident that He chose Paul and that one of his areas of expertise was entrepreneurship. If Paul's life is an example of what apostles, pastors, evangelists, and prophetic leaders should aspire to and desire, then entrepreneurship should be recognized or at least considered as a possible skill to be developed—not only in leaders of congregations but in lay members as well.

I'm sure that even Jesus as a youth was taught by Joseph (Mary's husband) to be a good carpenter. "Is not this the carpenter, the son of Mary...?" (Mark 6:3). I'm sure Joseph taught Jesus as he was growing up the entrepreneurial side of the carpentry business. In those days, the profession of the dad was traditionally handed down to the sons which is probably why Jesus' pre-ministry occupation was carpentry. My assumption behind that is Mary's husband Joseph was a carpenter.

In the next chapter, we will look at how money is made and mastered on a global scale and see what God's influence is in that process. Meanwhile, it is important to take a moment and reflect on the following point: Entrepreneurship and business in the life of Paul should not be taken lightly. Remember, that it was God's choice to use Paul and include his experience in business as part of his life.

CHAPTER 6

THE BIBLE AND WALL STREET

Before I begin to share how are there are biblical principles used by Wall Street, I must confess to you that these principles were taught to me by someone else. And, that person is my former mentor and role model, Leroy Cooper. However, the real credit for this lesson goes to S.B. Fuller. In my early days as a salesperson, I was a member of Mr. Cooper's sales organization. Mr. Cooper was mentored, taught, and trained by S.B. Fuller. The values and ideals that Leroy Cooper taught those of us in his sales force were in harmony with what he learned as a protégé of and salesman on S.B. Fuller's sales force. Every morning, Leroy would repeat quotes from Mr. Fuller. Leroy would assign us to read the books that Mr. Fuller read. The majority of the products that we sold were from Mr. Fuller's factory. The Fuller Products Company was the largest and most successful African American-owned business in the United States at that time. In the height of Mr. Fuller's achievement in 1960, he owned 13 businesses, employed 5,000 people, and had 125 locations across the nation.

In one of Mr. Fuller's sessions, as conveyed to us by Leroy Cooper who was there in training at the time in his early days as a sales representative, he shared with us who were in his sales organization some quite interesting information from a surprising source. The training session identified terminology used by Jesus in Matthew chapter 25, that is used on Wall Street today. The following words are found in the King James Version of Bible; "goods" (vs. 14), "traded" (vs. 16), "gained" (vs. 17), "money" (vs. 18), "exchangers" (vs. 27), "usury/interest" (vs. 27), and "profit / unprofitable" (vs. 30). Jesus walked the Earth more than 2,000 years ago, and here he is speaking these seven words that are some of the most common terms on today's stock market where stockbrokers and wealthy investors of modern times speak these words every day.

According to the *Encyclopedia Britannica*, Wall Street "is in the southern section of Manhattan in New York City, which has been the location of some of the chief financial institutions of the United States. The street is narrow and short and extends only about seven blocks from Broadway to the East River. It was named for an earthen wall built by Dutch settlers in 1653 to repel an expected English invasion." Wall Street is also synonymous to a large group of financial people and their power and policies (e.g. Black Wall Street in Tulsa Ok, in the early 1900s). It is an institution or organization having a public character just as a school, church, government, or bank has.

What is the prophetic relevance of these spoken words by Jesus who is knowledgeable of all things? Jesus knew that these words would be even more significant today in our modern economy than in the ancient times when he walked the Earth. I believe that by Jesus strategically and prophetically speaking about financial concepts, it affirms a message of hope to people of all generations for us to realize that even though we may have been born into poverty, if we use our talents, gifts, and abilities backed with strong desire and determination to get out of it, we can. We can because Jesus knows about finance, economics, achievement, and wealth. Deuteronomy 8:18 says, "But remember the Lord your God, for it is he who gives you the ability to produce wealth." God is the one who gives people and organizations the power to get wealth. God is the one who gives that innovative idea that can revolutionize life on planet earth. Edison's idea of the electric light was taboo to those that were stuck on using kerosene lamps for lighting. But with determination, ingenuity, and the flip of a switch, life on planet earth was changed forever. Edison was the inventor, but it took J.P. Morgan's money and insight to invest in his innovative idea.

It is vitally important to understand how financial markets operate. In my study of the stock market crash of 1929, I found out that people had been investing in stocks as if the value would never go down. When it did eventually drop, many banks failed. When the depositors heard about it, they panicked and went to the banks to get their money out. Ordinarily, this would not have been a problem because the deposits of the remaining customers would have covered those withdrawals. But, when the remaining depositors suddenly came and took their money also, that left the banks with nothing; so, they had to close. In 1931, 2,000 banks closed.

In 1933, 4,000 banks closed. Before that time, there was no federal deposit insurance. The majority of Americans were thrown into extreme poverty for about the following five years.

In 2008, a similar situation hit Wall Street. Unreasonable expectations that real estate prices could only go up, low interest rates from 2004 to 2005, and little-money-down mortgage loans motivated people to buy properties that the buyers couldn't afford. They bought the properties because they thought prices could only go up. In 2006, the price of homes started going down unexpectedly. Once Americans found out that selling their home would only produce prices that were of less value than their mortgage, they settled for foreclosure. The banks panicked when they saw that the rise in foreclosures would cause banks to lose money. This time, unlike 1929, most depositors didn't lose money by banks closing because of the Federal Deposit Insurance Corporation (FDIC). However, the homeowners lost the money they invested in their properties. What followed was investors' fear of loss; so, they stopped investing. Unfortunately, institutional racism played a major role in this because many national banks gave African American and other minorities home buyers subprime mortgage loans with fluctuating and or higher interest rates, which further exacerbated the foreclosure crisis. This caused a domino effect throughout the economy and led to a slow-down in manufacturing products, leading to massive layoffs. The layoffs combined with homeowners' spending cutbacks drove the economy into deep recession.

I believe that if the wealthy financial-management people had acknowledged God and asked for financial wisdom during the 1929 stock market crash and the 2008 recession, the downturns would have never happened. In both cases, God was speaking to Wall Street only for His voice to fall on deaf ears. I believe God wants our economy to be successful and advantageous to all of its citizens, rich and poor. However, if our economic leaders and average income earners refuse to ask Him for His advice, He won't provide it because He is the God who offers free will. He does not force Himself on His creation.

CHAPTER 7

GOD'S REVELATION TO ME ABOUT BUSINESS

In the past 25 years, there has been a routine I periodically perform in order to keep my mind in shape to do the work required in order to achieve my financial goals. I'll drive up to a spot about three miles from the downtown Loop area in Chicago and look over the skyline encompassing the sky-scraping buildings and say, "Today billions of dollars are going to exchange hands in this area, and some of it is going to come to me." Today, the direct-sales industry generates 182 billion dollars. Five percent of the people on Earth own all the wealth. The other ninety-five percent struggle to make their financial ends meet, or they engage in such strict spending guidelines that they actually sacrifice many things they really want to do for the sake of frugality or thriftiness.

What does Jesus have to say about this? In the parable of the talents (Matthew 25:14-31), the man going on the journey took the one talent from the wicked servant who was too lazy to invest it, and gave it to the servant who received five. Then, Jesus went further as if he knew the disciples were questioning why he gave the one talent to the servant who had received five instead of the servant who received two? In verse 29, Jesus says, "For to everyone who has, more shall be given, and he will have an abundance; but from the one who does not have, even what he does have will be taken away." There's that old saying, "The rich get richer and the poor get poorer." But let me expound on that a little more, "the wise get richer, but the foolish become impoverished and stay poor." This was true in the Lord's day and still has profound consequences today.

There are three reasons that I believe God gave me this revelation knowledge about money and its relationship with the church and the people of God, and I say this humbly. One, I'm not a proud or arrogant person. Two, I love sharing gained knowledge with people. And, three, I have a habit of asking God lots of questions. I remember one question I asked when I was around ten years old. I asked, "Why does a little boy my age have to work so hard to keep a few dollars in his pocket in order to buy something to eat when he is hungry?" Immediately, an answer came to me. It wasn't an audible voice I could hear but, instead, an inner voice in my consciousness that said, "People who own their own business live better than people who work on a job." This does not mean that they live better morally or that they don't have the same challenges in their family that employees have. It simply means that financially they have more options.

Fast-forward 50 years to a book titled The Business of the 21st Century by Robert Kiyosaki. He says, "A U.S. Federal

Reserve survey shows that the average household net worth for entrepreneurs is five times that of conventional employees. That means entrepreneurs are five times more likely to come out of this downturn and even stronger than before because they've created their own strong economy." The downturn" he's speaking of is the financial crisis the world experienced in 2008 when the real estate market crashed and the banks failed. Now, we will return to my boyhood years around 1960.

I believe that in my young innocence, with the purity of a child's heart and inquisitiveness of mind, God decided to treat my request for an answer as a prayer. And, He gave it to me right there on the spot. Wow, what a mighty God we serve! So, here's my childhood story. My dad worked for the U.S. Post Office. That was, as it is today, considered a good job. But, because there were my mother and seven children (five brothers, a sister, and I), we usually ran short of cash before my dad's next payday. During those times, about three days before payday, my mom would send me to the store with a handwritten note for Mr. Izzie, the local grocery-store owner. The note would ask for credit to buy food, stating that when Dad got paid he would pay the money. I'm sure Dad always paid because Mr. Izzie never denied us credit. Here Dad was working in that big building that took up several city blocks downtown with thousands of workers processing and delivering mail; yet, he always ran short of money before payday. And, here Mr. Izzie was with a small neighborhood store that would only hold a maximum of twelve people comfortably, but he could afford to extend credit to a customer in need.

I loved my dad, and I honor and respect him for the support he gave my mom and my siblings and me. It might sound like I'm bashing him in a demeaning way, but I'm not. He retired with 44 years' seniority, including the two years he was given for his time served in the U.S. Army overseas during World War II. Nor am I criticizing any of you who work on jobs or any of you who worked and are now retired. If Dad had known of a way to do better, he would have done better. He died shortly after retirement in 1987.

As a boy, I worked a paper route from 3:00 a.m. until 6:00 a.m. before school. After school, I worked for a preacher at his religious-goods store. On weekends, I assisted the subcontractor who was hired by the landlord of the building we lived in. My job was to help him as he made repairs and did maintenance work. Finally, at age sixteen, while in high school, I was able to get my first real job. However, my first business venture was an event that sparked a flame of desire in me to be a successful businessman. During the first three or four years, I noticed Christmas holiday-season activity in our store and other businesses. There was always a boost in sales. From November 1 to January 1, sales were up. But, on December 26, prices on everything everywhere dropped.

A money-making idea came to me. There was a display in the front of the store that had some baby dolls for sale. From November to December 25, they were $7.00 per doll. On December 26, I purchased 24 of them with my own money. The after-Christmas discount price to me was $2.50 per doll. After my shift, I walked out of the store with this big 3-1/2 feet wide, 4-1/2 feet tall box full of my business inventory. I awkwardly walked home, constantly shifting my box from side to side so I could see where I was going. I made it home in about five minutes since I only lived a block away. Once I got home, I cleared a space on the top shelf in the closet in our family apartment's hallway. I left them there for about 11 months. Then, on around December 1 the next year, I asked my manager if I could sell the dolls in front of the store on my day off. He said, "Yes." I sold them for $5.00 per doll. I made 100% profit.

After that event, I imagined what it would feel like to an infant cub who had only experienced the milk from its lioness mother's breast, who one day when he was mature enough tasted his first piece of meat. The smell of the fallen prey's blood on the grassy dinner table of the ground did something inside the cub, causing a shift in the cub's appetite. I had thought of, planned, initiated, and executed my first business deal. I believe it was at that point in my life, even though I didn't realize it at the time, that the blood of entrepreneurship started flowing in my veins. In the next chapter, I'll explain to you how God continued to reveal to me His views concerning business in my adulthood.

CHAPTER 8

God's Continued Revelation to Me about Business

There is a saying that I want to share with you. I believe this phrase and its application were the impetus or driving force to what was the next phase in my life leading to my development as a businessman and entrepreneur. Here it is: "When the student is ready, the teacher will appear."

In the previous chapter, I spoke of two businessmen, S.B. Fuller and Leroy Cooper. Around 1971, a lady who was a customer of the store where I worked saw something in me. Maybe it was the potential, hidden from me, to be a successful businessman. As it turned out, her son had a direct-sales business that facilitated daily sales meetings to which she invited me. Her name was Idella Cooper. Her son, Leroy Cooper, eventually became my mentor over a span of twenty-five years. As I said in chapter 6, Mr. Cooper was taught and trained by S.B. Fuller. Mr. Fuller was a business legend in his lifetime. He built a business legacy in Chicago and the nation that merits honor and respect.

In Mr. Cooper's daily sales meetings, we would receive training in sales techniques. We were taught the importance of business ownership and how the lack of it affects the living conditions in the community. We were shown the significance of individuals working for themselves as opposed to their working on a job for someone else. I don't believe it is wrong for a person to work as an employee on a job for someone else. I worked driving buses for twenty-five years for the Chicago Transit Authority. I retired with full benefits. However, there is a higher standard of vision among people who are employees and want more financially for themselves and their family. Remember the rich man from scripture named Zaccheus (Luke 19:1)? The Bible says that he worked as a "chief tax collector." With all that on-the-job responsibility as a Roman government tax collector, his job is comparable, with a little imagination, to a modern-day IRS agent. With whatever time-consumption quota he had to devote to his place of employment, he found time to own and operate a business. He evidently did a good job of balancing his job with his business time because the scripture says, "And he was rich."

What was his motivation to work his regular job plus additional hours as a businessman? Perhaps it was to create an inheritance for his family. If he had children, maybe he wanted more for them than what working on a job for the government would provide. Of course, the Bible doesn't state whether or not Zaccheus was married or had children. However, the example is there for us to examine, ponder, and implement if we so desire. This financial strategy is more available and easier for us today than in ancient times because of the many types of business models currently in use. We will examine these types in detail in a later chapter.

CHAPTER 9

MY APPLICATION OF GOD'S REVELATION TO ME ABOUT BUSINESS

In Mr. Cooper's daily sales meetings, we studied from a list of books that Mr. Fuller recommended to all of his salespeople across the country. They were the Bible, Think and Grow Rich by Napoleon Hill, The Secret of the Ages by Robert Collier, The Magic of Thinking Big by David J. Schwartz, The Power of Positive Thinking by Norman Vincent Peal, and many others. We were encouraged to go to our sales territories immediately after the meetings. Some weeks I did well, and others not so well. In our training, we were instructed to talk to 40 people every day. Of the 40, 21 of them, we hoped, would talk to us. Of that 21, 14 would place an order for a product for future delivery. The remaining seven would pay cash for their products. Our daily goal was to collect $70.00 per day in sales. This was called the "Twenty-One Forty Marketing Plan." This plan sounded good and simple. And, it was good and simple while we were sitting in those chairs in the meeting as the atmosphere of the room was charged with enthusiasm, energy, and excitement.

However, the challenge was the amount of discipline required to knock on 40 doors once you left the meeting and entered your territory alone. Walking the streets of my territory, facing fears of failure and rejection and doubts as to whether or not I would make any money were not easy demons to fight. Since I was not willing to stay out there and fight those fears and doubts in order to develop the skills and character necessary to become the entrepreneur that I needed to be in order to reach my financial goals, I quit selling and started looking for a job. The burden of being in business, developing a five-by-two city-block area seemed too heavy.

The next day, while I was in the downtown Chicago area searching for a job, I came across my aunt Mary. Now deceased, she was known in the family to be straightforward, strongly opinionated, solution oriented, and resourceful. Knowing she was the type of person she was, I told her that I was in the area looking for a job. This is what she said: "Now, Junior, I have a friend who is a bus driver. Go down to the Chicago Transit Authority (CTA) office tomorrow and fill out an application. Use my friend's name as a reference, and they will hire you." (Yes, my childhood name is "Junior," but you can call me "Eddie," thank you very much.) I then told her that I didn't have bus fare. She reached into her purse and gave me the money I needed for the trip. I went to the office the next day, filled out an application. Two weeks later, I was hired as a bus driver.

After I started driving and earning money as an employee of the CTA, I missed the participation with a prospective customer. I missed the challenge of finding out in conversation about his or her need and the value of my product's ability to satisfy that need. I'd go into a restaurant on my lunch break. While waiting in line for my turn to be served, I'd ask myself, "How many customers have to come into this establishment every day, and how much does each one have to spend for the owner to make a profit?" "Is it a franchise, or is it independently owned?" "Is the owner buying or renting this facility?" Every day when I pulled the bus into the bus garage to be serviced and parked, I would try to estimate the dollar amount the vault man emptied from the cash box into the huge vault that held the money from the buses. My eight-hour shift's worth of fare estimate was always equal to ten to 100 times more than what I was being paid each day. In most cities, before computerized fare boxes, cash was the form of passenger payment. After fourteen years of subtle torment, I decided to return to my business on a part-time basis.

Believe me, I was grateful for that salary from CTA, which is why I didn't quit that job. But, the training, knowledge, advantages of being a successful businessperson, wouldn't stop crying out from within me for fulfillment. So, I went back to my former sales force as a part-time salesperson and remained a city employee as a bus driver. My pattern and model was the biblical character Zaccheus who we discussed in chapter 4. The Bible says, "He was a chief tax collector and was wealthy" (Luke 19:1). This statement indicates that he probably balanced his tax-collecting job and business activities well. On his job, he attained the status of supervisor (in today's standard). In his business, he was recorded as wealthy.

About a month after I returned to the business of knocking on doors, re-establishing my customer list, and rebuilding a sales territory, I thought of an idea. The idea was for the company to create a department within the company that not only knocked on doors of family residences but also visited churches. The company could present an opportunity for the pastors and their congregation to earn a commission on a product in the company's inventory that every household could use. The particular product was a food flavor used for baking cakes, pies, and other foods. We offered vanilla, lemon, banana, pineapple, black walnut, and coconut. I presented the idea to Mr. Cooper. He liked it and gave the assignment to me. I went to the phone book and got the name, address, and phone number of 300 Chicago-area churches. Then, I created a letter of introduction. The letter was simple and short. Pastors and church leaders don't have a lot of free time. In the letter, I introduced the company, myself, the product, and the church's potential to earn 50 percent commission on their total sales. I mailed the letters. In a four-year period between 1991 and 1995, church fundraiser sales, according to my records, totaled a minimum of $10,000. At least three churches of the approximate 30 that were served did an average of $1,000 in sales.

Some time afterward, the company went out of business. Even though the doors of that particular business closed, my desire to help churches financially with available business opportunity still exists today in my heart. I prayed and asked God for another opportunity in the future to serve as a church fundraising entrepreneur. About 15 years later, He did just that.

CHAPTER 10

LUVENIA

I'd like to introduce you to a special lady. My friend, my lover, my wife, Luvenia. I met her and her youngest daughter, Angenique, on the bus route I was driving as a Chicago Transit Authority bus driver. The two of them were riding along with the rest of the seated load of passengers. Angenique and I thought it was funny because her mother was frantically digging in her purse to gather their fare while the money was the last thing on my mind. Luvenia was focused on her purse, and I was focused on Luvenia.

As I continued to drive what was then my favorite route on 75th Street from Damen Avenue to the lakefront on Chicago's Southside, I eventually picked up Luvenia again. This time, I got her phone number. I invited her to the sales training meetings that I attended. She said, "Yes." Next, I asked her to help me by becoming a member of my sales team of about five people. And, she said, "Yes." Finally, after three years of working together, I asked for her hand in marriage, and, again she said, "Yes."

Being in a marriage relationship with Luvenia sparked new life in me. To be with someone who believes in you and works day and night by your side in order to help you fulfill your dreams and financial goals is a very good thing. As I write these words, I find it challenging to find the right words to express the richness in dimension that she brought to my life.

When *Cooper Enterprises* went out of business, Luvenia and I started selling *Dudley Products* also. Joe Dudley was another one of Mr. Fuller's protégés. Mr. Dudley eventually built a successful manufacturing and retail business in Greensboro, North Carolina. On a *Cooper Enterprises*-sponsored business event, Luvenia and I along with a group of "Cooperites" from the Chicago area were invited to Mr. Dudley's luxurious mansion. He was a humble host as he talked to us about success and what we could do in our lifetime as a benefit of being hard-working entrepreneurs. One of our group members got a little nervous, this being the last day of the event, as our hotel check-out time was approaching. Mr. Dudley told us not to worry. The reason that he could afford to say that was because he owned the hotel that was accommodating us. In other words, if he told the Front Desk not to charge us for late check-out times, they would have to comply because they were his employees, and the facility where we were lodging belonged to him.

In those days, Luvenia used to put together some of the most beautiful gift baskets that a person could ever see. She would place Dudley and Fuller products in them along with teddy bears, combs, footie socks, or whatever would be useful to the customer that would complement the hair or skin-care products inside the basket package.

After 20 years of marriage, my Luvenia went home to be with the Lord. She departed from this life on January 28, 2017. The day before she passed, as she lay there in that terminally ill condition, I looked into her eyes and said, "I'm going to miss you when you're gone. Tell Jesus 'hello when you see him face-to-face. Tell him I'm coming but not now. I have more work to do. Tell him thanks for giving me more time and that I love him very much."

The next day when I came to visit her and exited the car, I heard the Holy Spirit say, "She's not in there, that's an empty shell." I pushed the message out of my mind and told myself it was for a future time but not today. I signed in at the front desk and walked through the secured doorway after being buzzed in. When I got to the nurse's station, the head nurse stepped forward and spoke the inevitable words that the Holy Spirit tried to prepare me for moments earlier. "Eddie, your wife passed." Both my bag on my left shoulder and my cap in my right hand hit the floor. I began to cry like a baby. I asked the nurse if I could see her. One of the attendants picked my things up off the floor and gave them to me. I walked into Luvenia's room and kissed her on the forehead.

Luvenia was a tough lady in life. I believe, with God's permission, she convinced death to wait until after the holidays because she wanted her daughters and me to get past 2016, her most challenging year. She didn't want our future to be tainted with the memory of her dying around Thanksgiving, Christmas, or New Year's Day. I think of her every day, thanking God for sharing one of his daughters with me through 20 years of marriage.

CHAPTER 11

KNOWING WHAT YOU WANT

I commend you for making it through the first ten chapters of this book, By now, you're probably feeling more empowered concerning your knowledge of God's feelings about your financial progress. That's good, and there is more to come.

Most people want to be able to pay their normal monthly expenses such as utilities (electricity and gas), phone, food, clothes, rent or mortgage, insurance, and transportation, just to name a few. I mentioned in an earlier chapter, the need for stored-up savings in case of an unexpected occurrence such as car or refrigerator breakdown. There are others who may want to finance their children's college education, save up enough for a down payment on a home, or take a dream vacation to a place on Earth they would really love to visit. Then, there are those who have a higher level of desire for their children and the following generations. Validation of the last group's desire is from God based on Proverbs 13:22 which says, "A good man leaves an inheritance to his children's children…." Incidentally, this scripture applies to good women also. This third group of men and women are people with higher vision. They see more than only benefit and comfort for themselves. They see posterity, which includes their descendants. For the scripture reference, we will look at Proverbs 29:18: "Where there is no vision, the people perish…" (KJV).

There are two things that I would like to point out about this group. One, they are not limited in their ability to think and dream big. To them, God is not in a box bound by dogmas, creeds, or religious beliefs. Two is that, even though they may be unaware of the fact, they have obeyed one of the first laws of success. They see what they actually want before they obtain it. And, just what is success? I've heard many interpretations. However, the one I've chosen and adopted for myself is from John Maxwell. He says: 1) "Success is knowing your purpose. 2) Growing to reach your maximum potential. 3) Sowing seeds to benefit others." His book is titled, *Your Road Map for Success*.

Now, let's reiterate an important point I've stated several times in previous chapters. You may be in one of the categories I previously spoke about who just want to pay your regular monthly expenses, children's college education, or buy a home. If that's you, don't worry about it, that's normal. Those of us who are Christians get the same promise—eternal life. However, if you are one of those people of God who want to leave some legacy financially, that's not pride or arrogance. If you love people, that's compassion. Generational curses of poverty have plagued many families for years and decades. Along with praying, fasting, and spiritual warfare, we must add the following: business knowledge, wisdom, the capacity to work hard, and love for people. In the next chapter, we will examine the advice of some experts on the subject of building wealth.

CHAPTER 12

WHAT MONEY-MAKING EXPERTS SAY
ABOUT MAKING MONEY

Richard Branson: "From my very first day as an entrepreneur, I've felt the only mission worth pursuing in business is to make people's lives better."

Warren Buffet: "Never depend on a single income, make investments to create a second source."

Jim Rohn: "Network marketing is the big wave of the future. It's taking the place of franchising which now requires too much capital for the average person."

Robert Kiyosaki: "Network marketing gives people the opportunity with very low risk and low financial commitment to build their own income generating asset and acquire great wealth."

As a young teen-ager, Richard Branson raised $8,000 soliciting businesses to advertise in a magazine he was producing. The cost of the magazine's production was $8,000. Then, he gave the magazines away for free to his fellow high-school friends. Now, let's analyze what just happened. He helped the businesses sell more products and services. Then, he helped the students by providing needed information concerning what's going on in their world. The key word in this venture description is *helped*. As he said in his own words, "I've felt the only mission worth pursuing in business is to make people's lives better." Jesus said in St. Luke 6:31, "Do to others as you would have them do to you." I believe and am in agreement with what motivational speaker and author Zig Ziglar said when he stated, "If you help enough people get what they want, you will by default get what you want." Living and working by these two principles, one from Jesus and one from Ziglar, are what got Branson to the multibillion-dollar status he now has.

Warren Buffet read his first book about buying and selling stocks when he was seven years old. As a young boy, he sold *Coca Cola* and chewing gum door to door. As an adult, he bought his first business, which was an old textile manufacturing plant about to close. He transformed it into a money-making establishment and invested in stocks of many other companies. Each business he acquired and each investment he made became an additional stream of income. Today Warren Buffet is wealthy-73 billion dollars strong.

Jim Rohn, who is now deceased, became a millionaire through a network-marketing company as an independent marketing representative. He was a motivational speaker and author. He wrote books on personal development and information concerning how to be successful in network marketing. His YouTube videos can still be visited on the internet. At the age of 25, he was broke. Six years later, after becoming involved in network marketing, he became a millionaire.

Jim says, "Network Marketing is … taking the place of franchising which now requires too much capital for the average person. Take a minute and think about two of the largest franchise restaurants in the world. One sells hamburgers and French fries, and the other sells sandwiches with a variety of meats in sub-sandwich style. If you were the owner of one of either of those stores you would have to pay millions of dollars to be one of their franchise owners. For a fraction of one percent of that cost, you could enroll in a network-marketing company with the possibility of earning the same or even more than some franchise-store owners.

Robert Kiyosaki is a business owner, motivational speaker, and author. Even though he didn't get his start through network marketing, he recommends it to people who want to build financial assets for themselves and their family. The two books of his that I'd like to recommend to you, my readers, are *Rich Dad Poor Dad* and *The Business of the 21st Century*. In the latter, he describes the dynamics and the advantages of being a network marketer.

Just what is *network marketing?* First of all, let's be clear, network marketing should not be confused with the illegal pyramid scheme *marketing,* where there is no real product being sold where the people on the top get rich off recruiting others under them. If no products, or services are being marketed or sold you have an unethical, and quite possibly, an illegal pyramid business.

However, *network marketing* is a system a company may use to distribute or market their goods and/or services. Instead of spending millions of dollars on billboard, television, and radio advertising, they pay the people who use the goods or services to spread the word. These companies pay a commission from the profits received back to the independent marketing agent. In most cases, the marketing representative is his or her very own best customer. Also, most network marketing companies promote their representatives to higher positions of pay when they introduce and sign up other people to become representatives.

By now, after twelve chapters of this book, you may feel a little overwhelmed. That's normal because, sometimes, in learning something new, a person has to unlearn some former things. For years, we as Christians have been involved in negative thinking when it comes to obtaining wealth and riches and the industry of network marketing. My hope is that the Holy Spirit uses the pages of this book to break the mindset of so many of us Christians who have doubts and fear when it comes to business and entrepreneurship...and network marketing.

CHAPTER 13

ELISHA, THE WIDOW, NETWORK MARKETING, AND YOU

In the book of II Kings, there is recorded an incident of a woman whose husband died. He left an unpaid financial debt which she inherited from him at his passing. During his lifetime, he was a member of an association of prophets. The biblical historian Josephus and another bible commentator identify the woman's husband as Obadiah, Ahab's chief steward. Jezebel, Ahab's wife, was on a murderous killing spree of the Lord's prophets. Obadiah saved one hundred of these prophets by hiding them in two caves (I Kings 18:4). Before he died, he borrowed money to feed those prophets while they were hiding. Now that he was deceased, his creditor was coming to take Obadiah's children to be slaves to satisfy the unpaid debt. This type of arrangement was common in this era. It was business, and it was legal.

It is very interesting how the prophet Elisha assisted and ministered to the woman's need. She needed money to pay off her husband's debt that was left to her. In fact, if she didn't come up with the money, she would lose custody of her children and have to hand them over to her creditor as slaves. They would probably have to live the rest of their lives in bondage. Let's take a look at the scripture from II Kings 4:1-7.

> The wife of a man from the company of prophets cried out to Elisha, "Your servant my husband is dead, and you know that he revered the Lord. But now his creditor is coming to take my two boys as his slaves." Elisha replied to her, "How can I help you? Tell me what do you have in your house?" "Your servant has nothing at all," she said, "except a little oil." Elisha said, "Go around and ask all your neighbors for empty jars. Don't ask for a few. Then, go inside and shut the door behind you and your sons. Pour oil into all the jars, and as each is filled, put it to one side." She left him and afterward shut the door behind her and her sons. They brought the jars to her, and she kept pouring. When all the jars were full, she said to her son, "Bring me another one." But, he replied, "There is not a jar left." Then the oil stopped flowing. She went and told the man of God, and he said, "Go, sell the oil and pay your debts. You can live on what is left." (NIV)

Here are the main points: 1) Her "... little oil" was all Elisha and God needed to work her miracle. 2) Her asking for help from her neighbors and their cooperation in lending her their empty jars was necessary. 3) The size of her faith and intensity of her determination produced the number of jars she received. 4) The shutting of the door sheltered her and her sons from the noise and distractions of the outside world so that they could stay focused on what they were told to do. 5) After they had done the things that the prophet told them to do, she reported back to Elisha, and he gave her their final instruction. "Go, sell the oil and pay your debts. You and your sons can live on what's left."

My question is, and maybe yours also, Why didn't God just rain down the money from the sky on to her front lawn? He had already miraculously produced such a large overflow of oil from only one original vessel to fill up hundreds or even a thousand or more containers. After all, He is God, and He possesses all power. I believe the answer is that He wanted her to be a part of her own miracle. He had two parts for her to play: collecting the jars and selling the oil. Not only was the value of the oil enough to pay off their debt. It was also enough for her and her boys to live on.

Let's look at some miracles and consider the part the recipient plays in each. When God delivers an alcoholic, he has to stop going into bars and lounges. When God delivers a man from sexual addiction, he has to stop viewing pornographic materials. When God delivers a woman from prostitution, she has to stop offering her body for money. When God delivers a racist (black or white) from racism, he or she has to stop being prejudiced against people based on skin color or nationality. When God delivers a murderer from committing more murders, he or she has to stop degrading the value of human life. So, consequently, when God delivers a person from poverty, he or she has to stop waiting on prosperity to come but instead must go obtain and embrace the wisdom and knowledge to receive it.

This is what the widow did through the power of the Holy Spirit that was upon the prophet Elisha. Not only did she receive enough to pay off her debt, which saved her children from slavery. But, she also received enough to live on. Suppose she had collected more vessels from her neighbors? She would have received even more miraculous overflow of oil and would have been able to provide an even better life for herself and her sons. But, according to the amount of faith reflected in the amount of jars collected, she received in direct proportion to the intensity and depth of her belief.

The widow in this story needed money to pay off debt and pay for living expenses. So do most of us in this 21st century. In Matthew 6:25, Jesus mentions food, clothes, and something to drink because they are essentials. With His being both God and man, He also knew that we would need, in this day and age, electricity, gas (utilities), mortgage or rent, cell or home phone service, transportation costs (automobile or public transportation), refrigerator, television, stove, insurances, and other things, depending on the circumstances of the family—things such as children's education, child care, internet service, etc.

This pattern of solution that God through Elisha provided for the widow is an example of what the industry of network marketing can provide for a person or a family. The fact is big name franchise businesses cost hundreds of thousands and even millions of dollars to start. Here is a list of similarities between the widow's solution in the Bible and present-day network marketing:

1) The average start-up fee ranges from $100 to $500. That's little compared to traditional businesses.

2) You obtain cooperation of friends to help you by using your company's goods and/or services. Also, bonuses and extra commissions are earned when you sign someone up to join your team.

3) The size of your faith and its corresponding application determine the number of friends you solicit.

4) Due to the negativity and non-belief of many friends and relatives concerning this industry, you shut the door of your thinking and focus on goals, desires, training, and belief concerning what it is you have to do.

Am I saying that this chapter is a Biblical example of what Network Marketing is? My answer is no. But I am saying that many of the circumstances and principals are similar.

CHAPTER 14

AN INTERVIEW WITH DAVE SILVERMAN

I would like to introduce you to a friend of mine. He is also a business partner of which I happen to be in his organization. Within our group he has experienced an enormous amount of success and is now ranked to an executive level of leadership among the independent marketing representatives of our team. I respect him not only for his achievements and leadership, but also for his common touch and connection of love he has for all his followers under his hierarchy, as well as those on his level and above. The following is an interview where he graciously answered several questions of which I'd like to share his insightful answers with you.

1) How long have you been a Network Marketer and why did you join this industry?

Answer; I joined over 20 years ago. I went to a good school, had a good job, but my income was limited. A friend approached me about the business. I asked him, "What kind of scam is this?" The only reason I went [to his presentation] was to show him the problems of it and prove it was a scam. However, I couldn't find it [flawed]. After the presentation my friend took me up to the speaker who I told,"Honestly,

I came to shoot this opportunity down but I can't find any-thing wrong with it, it sounds like a good business". Then the speaker asked me, "Do you see an opportunity for your-self?" I said, "No, I have a good job and a good salary". Then he asked me, "Do you pay a lot in taxes?" He went on to show me how the business would help me save money on taxes. So I joined for the tax benefits. I went to some of my friends. They weren't interested in the business but they joined for the tax savings. That five friends I got to join the business blossomed into 125,000 plus 100,000 customers.

2) What were the main challenges you had to push through in order to establish yourself as a profes-sional Network Marketer?

Answer: *Attitude*, I had to get over my stigmas. I was a snob. I thought it was a legitimate business, but for someone else. I was only looking at the tax benefits. *Mindset*, I had the mindset of an employee. You go to work and put in a cer-tain amount of hours and get a certain amount of dollars. As an entrepreneur the mindset has to be different. I had to get things right in my head. *Negative People*. One of the first people I called [to prospect] was my Mom. She asked me was I crazy? Friends and family were the worst [critics]. They fear you stepping up and out because you might leave them behind. My Dad worked for Kodak and my Mom was a teacher. She also ran the family business. They never made more than sixty or seventy thousand dollars per year. You can make that amount of money in one month in this in-dustry. This business is a growth journey. It's not a sprint, it's a marathon. In this business it takes time to succeed. To overcome challenges in this business you must remove your mental blocks, develop your business and people skills, and keep your mental vision of where you are taking yourself and your business.

3) Did you ever have doubts about your ability to succeed in this industry?

Answer: I was in this business for one year 9 times before I did my 2nd year. I've always had doubts about this industry. There have been times when it was uncomfortable. Being out in the field and not having made any money in a week or in a month. You think about how easy it would be to get yourself another job where all you have to do is show up and get paid for every hour you work. But I knew it was a learning curve I had to continue to embrace. I have two people who ride on my shoulders all the time. On the left is Lazy Dave. He believes in putting in the normal amount of effort. The one on my right shoulder is Rich Dave. He's the driving force within me. He pushes me to the "Why" I do this business. Lazy Dave on the left shoulder is consumed by an employee mentality. Rich Dave on the right shoulder is driven by the Boss mentality.

In our [company compensation plan] leadership position that I hold, I had a slow month during December. We made money, but we didn't have a lot of meetings. I could have done more. It took me eight and a half years to reach my first executive leadership position. It took me another ten years to promote to the next highest position. The reason I'm successful is because I didn't quit.

Everyone has doubts. The answer is a strong support system. There is someone here [in your organization] who is willing to help you. On a job you don't want anyone to know what you know. Here I want my team member to promote and replace me.

4) What advice would you give to a person who is considering becoming a Network Marketer?

Answer: 1) Don't listen to unqualified people. If you wanted your son or daughter to be a good basketball player, who would you suggest they listen to Micheal Jordan or Uncle Bubba? 2) Selling is a service to people. Don't sell a product you don't believe in and don't sell for a company that you don't believe in. 3) Commit to sticking with the business. Many obstacles will confront you in this business. Some people have a bad experience and quit. 4) Have a strong work ethic. Find something that motivates you and focus on it as you work your business. 5) Become a student of the game. Master your skill and craft. 6) Stay plugged in to your company's system and leadership. Take notes during trainings and utilize outside trainings.

5) How likely would a person with no Network Marketing experience be able to reach a high level of achievement?

Answer: That's like asking, "How likely can a man lift a two hundred pound weight if he comes to the gym for 2 years". Or, "How likely would you expect someone to lose weight if they go on a diet." A person's achievement is based on their own determination.

In America, we are quitters. Gym membership is high in the beginning of the year, but 2 months later [it falls off].

6) Does the current pandemic crisis present an advantage or disadvantage to starting and maintaining a Network Marketing business?

Answer: Anytime is a good time for Network Marketing. It gives the ability to work a business from home without face-to-face contact, instead through technology and mail.

Jobs are not stable. Even if your job leaves and comes back, it can leave again. Tax benefits are available [to business owners that employees don't qualify for]. Who would pay more if they didn't have to? Also, the requirements of corporate America's [work force differ from the Network Marketing industry]. You can have a record [of past jail or prison time] and in Network Marketing you won't be discriminated against. Your achievement is based on your [current performance] instead of your past.

7) How has your current Network Marketing Opportunity fulfilled your desire to help so many people?

Answer: I've always been a person who wants to help people. Some of us want more for others than what they want for themselves. I moved back to Rochester New York to help my Mom and Dad. Network Marketing is a gift to people. Just [an extra] one hundred dollars a month would help a lot of people.

The relationships I've acquired, the people I've met, and the growth I've experienced has made me a better person. Now my goal is to bless as many people that want to be blessed.

I have a friend who sells baseball cards on Amazon. I would build his business for him. Because of his mental state he can't do the business right now.

I get more excited seeing other people succeed. I took my daughters fishing and I caught a large fish. They caught some small sun fishes. The joy on their faces was so enjoyable to me.

8) What advice would you give to faith leaders(Christian, Jewish, or Islamic) about how Network Marketing can benefit them and their congregations?

Answer: Faith people think Network Marketing people are like wolves in sheep clothing. They think Network Marketers are coming to cheat them.

When a Network Marketer comes to you, have faith, open your mind, and heart. And to the Network Marketers reading this, be sincere and honest-not salesy or pushy. The point is, that will cause people to find reason not to believe you. If God brings a Network Marketing strategy and plan, it's a blessing.

Remember the story of the two sets of foot prints in the sand. The person asked the Lord, "Why is it that when things got bad on the journey I only see my one set of footprints instead of yours and mine, did you abandon me?" The Lord answered, "No, When the journey got too bad for you to bear I carried you. That's why during the hard times you see only one set of footprints, mine."

Then there's the story of the man who asked the Lord to save him from the flood. While the water was only ankle deep rescuer's came to his home knocking on his door saying, "The water is rising, come get in the truck and we'll get you to safety." The man replied, "No, I prayed and the Lord said He would save me." Then the flood water rose up to the second floor of the man's house. Rescuer's came by in a boat and yelled through the window saying, "The water is rising, come get in the boat and we'll get you to safety." The man replied, "No, I prayed and the Lord said He would save me." Finally, the water engulfed the entire house except for a spot on the roof. This time rescuer's came along in a helicopter. They dropped a rope to the man and yelled, "Grab the rope and climb up and we'll take you to safety. The man looked up and shouted back, "I prayed to the Lord and He said He would save me." Then the water rose ten feet above the roof. Before the man lost consciousness and drowned he was able to ask God why He didn't save him. God replied, "I sent you a truck, a boat, and a helicopter."

You have to recognize that God often answers prayer in practical ways. We can't always look for some spectacular miraculous intervention. Remember, as I stated earlier, God wants you to be part of the miracle. Believing God often means you have to believe that God is going to use you in the process. Therefore, *you* have to sell your business. *You* have to sell yourself to others. And in the process we're giving people a blessing which opens the door to your blessing, all to the glory of God and His kingdom.

CHAPTER 15

AN INVITATION TO SALVATION

I suppose that there are some of you who don't have a relationship with Christ. Maybe you read this book up to this sentence because the title attracted you and you wanted to learn more about God's relationship between the church and network marketing. You may have noticed that throughout this book, I have used the term *born again* and the word *Christian*. The term *born again* comes from a statement Jesus made in the Bible in St. John 3:7, "You must be born again." The word *Christian* was the name that the people of the community of Antioch gave to the followers of Christ: "The disciples were called Christians first at Antioch" (Acts 11:26).

The book of Ezekiel 18:4, declares a statement through one of His Prophet's; "For every living soul belongs to me, the father as well as the son-both alike belong to me. The soul that sins is the one who will die." This death the prophet is speaking of is a spiritual death. Yes we all will die physically. However, when a human being is existing without the a relationship with God through the finished work of Jesus on the cross they are separated from God (which is a type of death). That's where a rebirth comes in. This is a provision God has provided through the sacrifice of His son Jesus.

I would like to take some time and share with you how I became a born-again Christian. But, before I do that, I'd like to explain from a biblical perspective the meaning of Jesus's phrase "born again." The apostle Paul mentions in his writing to the Thessalonian Church three divisions of a person. "May your whole spirit, soul and body be kept blameless [protected and finished] at the coming of our Lord Jesus Christ" (I Thessalonians 5:23). The spirit is the innermost part of a person's being or existence. The soul is a combination of a person's emotions, will, and intellect. The body is the physical part of us. At birth or conception, the spirit and soul unite and inhabit the body as a result of procreation. When a person is born again, the spirit is re-created by the work of the Holy Spirit and made new, which is why Jesus called it being "born again." "I say to you, unless one is born again he cannot see the kingdom of God" (John 3:3b). This newly re-created, Holy Spirit-designed human spirit on the inside of a person affects them in a positive way concerning the emotions and will. It even promotes better thinking patterns if the person practices the discipline of applying God's word from the Bible into their thinking process. It can also produce physical healing in our body through the power of the blood that Jesus shed on the cross.

When I was at the age of nineteen, my younger brothers Tyrone, Bruce, and Reggie led me on my path to know God through the work that Christ did along with the sacrifice that he made of himself on the cross. After they became

Christians receiving the new birth, I observed a newly found joy and peace they suddenly had. We all lived in the same house which allowed me the opportunity to see their life up close. About two months after they received Christ into their life, I decided that I wanted that new life they were experiencing. So, I received him into my life, repented of my sins, and began a new life in him.

If you want that new life that only Christ can give, you can have it right now. It's very simple. Just repeat these few words, "Lord, I [your name] ask you to come into my life right now. Forgive me for every sin I committed. Thanks for birthing me into your family through Jesus Christ. Amen!" Romans 10:9 says, "That if you confess with your mouth, Jesus is Lord, and believe in your heart that God raised him from the dead, you will be saved." Let me be the first person to welcome you into God's family. It's important now that you find a church that believes the Bible so you can learn, grow, and share your new life with others. If you ask him, he will help guide you to one.

CHAPTER 16
PAULETTE

I would like to introduce you my readers to a very classy lady I met at a company weekly business meeting. Over time we developed a platonic friendship. At the time Paulette and I developed our friendship I was involved with another woman of whom we had seriously talked about marriage. You may remember in chapter ten of this book I became a widower after the death of my former wife, Luvenia. At that time in prayer, I told God, "I'm going to wait 2 years before I consider starting an intimate relationship with someone else." The interesting thing about God is that when we, his servants tell him what we are going to do, he sometimes responds in ways we never expect. This was the case with me. After telling him about my proposed two year wait before thinking about another relationship he responded, "Yes, but I'm going to shorten that two year period."

Due to some health challenges of mine my fiancé thought it best for us not to talk about our marriage plans. I was devastated at her decision, but I understood. I do not hold it against her because a person has a right to accept or reject entry of another person's presence in their life, especially in a matter as intimate as marriage.

Two days later I talk to Paulette about what happened. As she shared my pain and allowed me to cry on her shoulder I looked into her eyes and saw my wife. I suddenly realized that our past two years of friendship was an introduction of her into my life into the role she was meant to play. And that role was to be that of my wife. We married four months later, one year and eleven months after the passing of Luvenia.

Network Marketing has been good to me. It helped me during the passing of my former wife, with purposeful work to do. It provides me a tool to help others who need a way to replace lost income. And it supplied me with a wife. My hope is that you, who may be afraid to join a Network Marketing company to at least now consider the possibilities. I highly recommend that you pick up a copy of one of the books in my Recommended Book List following this chapter. Robert Kiyosaki's *The Business of The 21st Century* or John C Maxwell's *The Power of Five* are excellent choices. Those two books go into more detail about the the subject of Network Marketing. So until we meet again in print or in person on this journey of shared information, I wish, hope, and pray for each of you to fulfill your God given purposes in life and that each of you allow Him to bless you in this thing we call life.

RECOMMENDED READINGS

Rich Dad, Poor Dad by Robert Kiyosaki

Business of the 21ˢᵗ Century by Robert Kiyosaki

Entrepreneur Roller Coaster by Darren Hardy

Redefining the American Dream by Thomas Felder

You Can, You Will by Joel Osteen

Thousands by John Eckhardt

Success Is Not An Accident by Tommy Newberry

How To Get Out Of Debt by James Meeks

The Power Of Five and *Your Road Map to Success* by John C. Maxwell

About the Publisher

Let *Life to Legacy* bring your story to literary life! We offer the following publishing services: manuscript development, editing, transcription services, ghost-writing, cover design, copyright services, ISBN assignment, worldwide distribution, and eBook conversion.

We make the publishing process easy. Throughout production, we keep the author informed every step of the way. Even if you do not have a manuscript, that's not a problem for us. We can ghost-write your book from audio recordings or legible handwritten documents. Whether print-on-demand or trade publishing, we have packages to meet your publishing needs. At *Life to Legacy*, we take the stress out of becoming a published author.

Unlike other *so-called* publishers, we do more than just print books. Our books and eBooks are distributed to book buyers, distributors, and online retailers throughout the world. This is real publishing! Call us today for a free quote.

Please visit our website
www.Life2Legacy.com

or call us
877-267-7477

Send email inquiries to
Life2Legacybooks@att.net